D1549493

First published 2002

ISBN 0 7110 2902 4

All rights reserved. No part of this book may be reproduced or
transmitted in any form or by any means, electronic or mechanical,
including photocopying, recording or by any information storage
and retrieval system, without permission from the Publisher in
writing.

© Ian Allan Publishing Ltd 2002

Published by Ian Allan Publishing

an imprint of Ian Allan Publishing Ltd, Hersham, Surrey
KT12 4RG.
Printed by Ian Allan Printing Ltd, Hersham, Surrey KT12 4RG.

Code: 0204/A

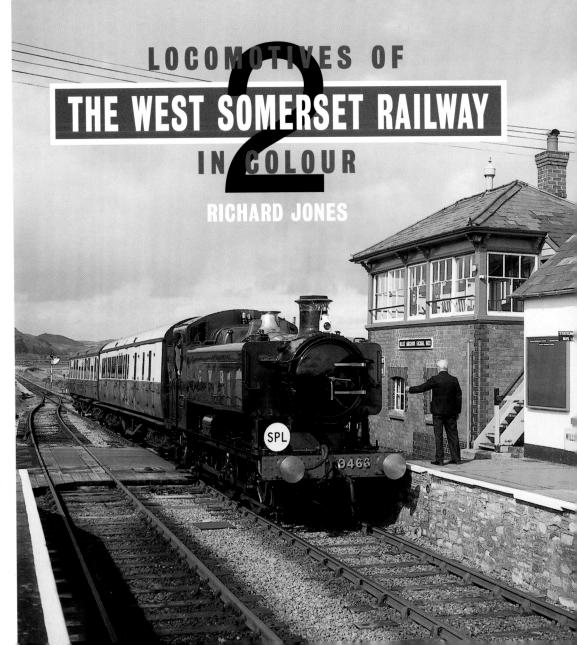

LOCOMOTIVES OF
THE WEST SOMERSET RAILWAY
2
IN COLOUR

RICHARD JONES

Front cover: GWR 'Hall' class 4-6-0 No 4920
Dumbleton Hall passes the edge of the beach soon
after departing from Blue Anchor station with the
4.05pm Bishops Lydeard–Minehead train on
14 August 1997. *Bryan Hicks*

Back cover: LMS Ivatt 2-6-2T No 41312 steams
past Nethercott, between Crowcombe Heathfield
and Bishops Lydeard, with a special charter train on
18 March 1999 recreating the days of the West
Country branch milk train. *Don Bishop*

Right: GWR '94xx' class 0-6-0PT No 9466 coasts
into Blue Anchor station with a typical branch-line
local train formed of two Great Western coaches.
The fireman is about to surrender the single-line
token to the signalman. *David J. Williams*

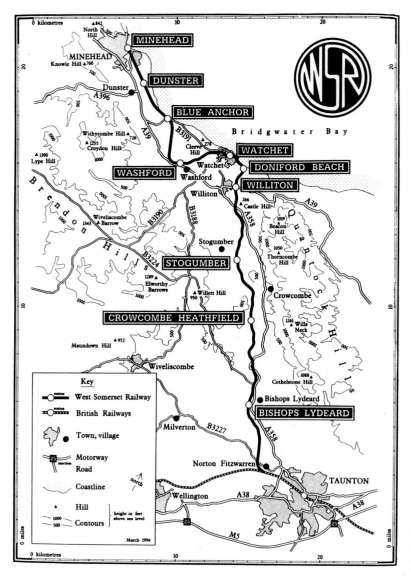

Key

station○	West Somerset Railway
station×	British Railways
	Town, village
25	Motorway Junction
	Road
	Coastline
▲	Hill
1000	height in feet above sea level
500	Contours

March 1994

Introduction

The West Somerset Railway is now firmly established as one of the finest and most successful independent heritage railways in Britain, and one of the most popular visitor attractions in the West of England. The former Taunton–Minehead branch was reopened in 1976 and therefore has now celebrated its 25th anniversary of passenger-train operation. In recent years the WSR has enjoyed unprecedented success, with over 169,000 passengers travelling on the line in 2001 alone.

The WSR runs for 20 miles between Minehead, on the Bristol Channel coast, and Bishops Lydeard, just five miles from Taunton, the county town of Somerset, on which regular passenger trains operate, and for a further three miles southwards to Norton Fitzwarren, where the branch enjoys a connection with the West of England main line. Running through some of the finest scenery in the West Country, ranging from the coastal plain and beaches of Blue Anchor Bay to the Quantock Hills, the WSR possesses a unique Great Western branch-line atmosphere, which has been further enhanced in recent years.

Regular timetabled passenger services, mostly steam-hauled, operate between Minehead and Bishops Lydeard throughout most of the year, and are supplemented by a number of high-profile special events each season that are becoming increasingly popular. In addition, the section south of Bishops Lydeard to Norton Fitzwarren has continued to see an increasing amount of use at special events, with charter trains (both steam and diesel) from the national network and commercial freight traffic, including the transport of over 100,000 tonnes of stone for two sea defence schemes in the area. Over the last 25 years a tremendous variety of locomotives, both steam and diesel, has worked on the WSR.

The first volume of *Locomotives of the West Somerset Railway* (published in early 1997) featured at least one photograph of all the locomotives that had worked a passenger train between Minehead and Bishops Lydeard in the preservation era between 1976 and 1996. This second volume not only continues that theme, but extends it! As well as bringing the story up to date by including a photograph of all the steam and heritage diesel locomotives that have worked a passenger train on the WSR between 1997 and 2001 (inclusive), this book also includes a number of other events that have featured on the line over this period, including through charter trains from the main-line network and the commercial stone traffic. Clearly, in the case of the latter, it has not been possible to include a photograph of every locomotive involved! In addition, there are also photographs of some WSR-based engines which since 1997 have appeared in different liveries.

Two things are apparent when looking at the portfolio of photographs in the two volumes of *Locomotives of the West Somerset Railway*. Firstly, over the 25 years since the WSR reopened, a tremendous variety and number of locomotives have worked on the line. This has been possible largely because of the railway's commitment to upgrading and maintaining the infrastructure of the line and the willingness of owners to see their locomotives in action on the WSR. Secondly, it is doubtful whether there would have been sufficient material to fill even one book, let alone two, were it not for the Barry scrapyard phenomenon. Most of the steam engines that have worked over the branch since 1976 were rescued from the famous South Wales scrapyard, before being restored to steam to enjoy a new lease of life in preservation. The WSR and, indeed, almost every other heritage steam railway, has much to be thankful for to the owners of the former scrapyard for postponing their demise on several occasions!

As in the first volume, the photographs portray the beauty of the scenery along the line in all four seasons, and feature a wide variety of locations and trains. Once again, no excuse is offered for conveying the impression that the sun always seems to shine in West Somerset!

Acknowledgements

Many people contributed material for consideration for publication in this book, to whom the author is extremely grateful. Choosing the photographs to ensure a good balance of locomotives, trains and locations was no easy task. The author would also like to express his thanks to John Pearce and the Directors of the West Somerset Railway Association for their support.

Richard Jones
Milverton, Somerset
January 2002

Right: The author enjoys a driving turn on LNER 'B1' No 61264. *Bob Robson*

Spring sunshine

Left: BR Class 4 2-6-4T No 80136 makes a fine sight as it climbs passes near Old Cleeve on the climb from Blue Anchor to Washford on 23 December 2001. No 80136, built by British Railways at Brighton Works in 1956, made two visits to the WSR in 2001, becoming the first member of the class to have ever worked over the Minehead branch. The 'Standard tank' proved ideally suited to working passenger trains on the line, and its visit was very well received by visitors, photographers and engine crews! *Don Bishop*

Branch-line local

Right: BR(W) '5101' class 2-6-2T No 4160 — the first of the final batch of 20 engines actually built by British Railways at Swindon in 1948/9 to a Great Western design — coasts downhill towards Watchet with the 1.45pm Williton–Minehead during the WSR's Spring Steam Gala on 24 March 2000. No 4160 was returned to steam in August 1993, after undergoing an extensive restoration at Minehead, and since then has become one of the most regular and reliable members of the WSR steam fleet, achieving a total mileage in excess of 70,000 by the end of 2001. After five years running in BR lined black livery, No 4160 was turned out in unlined Brunswick green and lettered 'British Railways' in GWR sans-serif style — as it was when built — as seen in the photograph. *Richard Jones*

HOGWARTS EXPRESS
WEST COUNTRY CLASS

The 'Hogwarts Express'

Left: One of the former Southern Railway 'West Country' class engines designed by O. V. S. Bulleid, No 34027 *Taw Valley*, has made two extremely successful 'guest' visits to the West Somerset Railway. During its second visit, in 2000, the engine appeared in red and was renamed *Hogwarts Express* following a promotional tour around the country to publicise the fourth of J. K. Rowling's popular books about the young wizard Harry Potter — *Harry Potter and the Goblet of Fire*. Many people of all ages visited the WSR especially to see and travel behind No 34027. The Bulleid Pacific departs from Stogumber with a Bishop Lydeard-bound train. *Ken Steel*

Inset: A close-up of the *Hogwarts Express* nameplate on the left-hand running plate of No 34027, in the same style as the place-names originally applied to the 66 'West Country' members of the 110-strong class. *Richard Jones*

High Speed Train

Right: Minehead has become a very popular destination for charters from the main-line network in recent years, and a wide variety of locomotives, both steam and diesel, have worked passenger trains on the WSR as a result. Several High Speed Train sets have worked over the line, the first such visit occurring on 16 January 1993. During the Autumn Steam Gala, on 12 September 1999, a First Great Western-liveried HST set stands in the bay platform at Minehead station. *Richard Jones*

Commercial freight

Above: In conjunction with national rail-freight operator English, Welsh & Scottish Railway, the WSR secured a contract to carry stone for use in the building of a new sea defence scheme at Minehead. EWS locomotives — principally 'heavyweight' Class 37/7s — from Westbury were used to transport stone from two quarries in the Mendips (Merehead and Whatley) throughout to Minehead, working over the WSR's connection with the West of England main line at Norton Fitzwarren.

The first train, hauled by No 37711, ran on 24 March 1997 and between then and 15 June 1998 — the date of the final loaded train — 106,000 tonnes of stone was delivered to Minehead as part of the contract. No 37715 passes through beautiful West Somerset scenery at Nethercott, on the climb to Crowcombe Heathfield, with a loaded train. *Peter Vile*

After a storm

Right: One of the attractions at the March 2000 Spring Steam Gala was the operation of GWR 'Castle' class 4-6-0 No 5051 *Earl Bathurst*, normally based at Didcot Railway Centre — the second member of the class to have traversed the Minehead branch. In a patch of sunshine set against a threatening sky, No 5051 approaches Nornvis Bridge, south of Crowcombe Heathfield, on 25 March 2000 with the 11.40am Norton Fitzwarren–Minehead. *Don Bishop*

Magnificent Mogul

Left: Between the introduction of the class in 1911 and its closure in October 1964, Taunton shed played host to many of the GWR '43xx' class 2-6-0 tender engines. These were used regularly on the branches to Barnstaple and Minehead. One of only two preserved members of the once 342-strong class, No 7325, built as No 9303 at Swindon Works in 1932, is based on the Severn Valley Railway, and has made three visits to the WSR in recent years — for the Spring Steam Galas in 1997, 1999 and 2000. During its second visit, on 19 March 1999, the Collett Mogul recreates a previous era as it passes Bye Farm (between Watchet and Washford) with the 2.15pm Bishops Lydeard–Minehead. The tower of St Decuman's Church, Watchet, can be seen on the hill in the right background. *Don Bishop*

Around the curves

Right: Another popular 'guest' engine at WSR Steam Galas in recent years has been GWR '94xx' class 0-6-0PT No 9466. Designed by the last Chief Mechanical Engineer of the Great Western, F. W. Hawksworth, 210 members of the class were built between 1947 and 1956, mostly by outside contractors. Their life expectancy was short from the outset — quickly being replaced with diesels by British Railways — and they were withdrawn whilst still having low mileages and many years of useful life left in them. No 9466, which was built in February 1952 and withdrawn by BR in March 1965, has made four very successful visits to the WSR between 1999 and 2001. In glorious spring sunshine, No 9466 rounds the curves at Nethercott as it descends to Bishops Lydeard with the 2.20pm from Minehead on 19 March 1999. *Mark Wilkins*

On test

Above: During the summer of 1996, Rail Express Systems used the WSR — principally the section between Bishops Lydeard and Norton Fitzwarren — for driver training purposes to test a possible future 'push-and-pull' system using a Class 47 diesel locomotive and a rake of postal vans, with a newly-converted 'Propelling Control Vehicle' (PCV) at the end of the set. In matching liveries, No 47733 *Eastern Star* and PCV No 94315 pause just south of Bishops Lydeard during the trials on 22 August 1996. Exactly a week earlier, No 47733 had become the first Class 47 locomotive to reach Minehead. *Richard Jones*

'Small Prairie' at night

Right: During the 1999 Autumn Steam Gala a 'night shoot' for photographers was organised at Dunster station, using GWR '4575' class 2-6-2T No 5541, normally based at the Dean Forest Railway. This was the engine's second visit to the WSR that year. No 5541 makes a superb sight posed outside the restored station goods shed — now the base of the railway's Permanent Way Department — on 11 September 1999. *Don Bishop*

Past the pillboxes

Above: GWR 'Hall' class 4-6-0 No 4936 *Kinlet Hall*, a West Country-based engine between April 1940 and May 1962, passes Ker Moor, between Dunster and Blue Anchor, with the 2.45pm Minehead–Bishops Lydeard on 1 April 2001, the third day of the Spring Steam Gala. Restored to main-line condition — and based — at Tyseley Locomotive Works in Birmingham, No 4936 was one of six 'guest' engines at this event. The train is about to pass two former World War 2 pillboxes — there are several visible along this stretch of line — and the photograph illustrates well the fact that, at present, WSR engines spend half their time running 'backwards'! *Alan Randle*

Delivering the goods

Right: A 'new' engine that made its debut on the WSR in 2001, after restoration from scrapyard condition which was completed at Minehead, was GWR '42xx' class 2-8-0T No 4247, built originally in 1916 primarily to work short-haul heavy coal trains from the pits to the steelworks and docks in South Wales. During the Autumn Steam Gala, No 4247 leaves Stogumber with the 8.50am ex Minehead demonstration goods train on 16 September 2001. *Don Bishop*

Maybach music

Above: For several months in 2000, one of the members of the well-liked 'Western' class of ex-British Railways Western Region diesel-hydraulic locomotives — No D1023 *Western Fusilier* — was based on the WSR. Built at Swindon Works in September 1963, No D1023 was one of the most popular members of the once 74-strong class in later years, being the last 'Western' to receive a major overhaul at Swindon, the last member of the class to receive the dual-braking conversion, the only 'Western' to carry 'domino' front end indicator panels, and (together with

No D1013 *Western Ranger*) it worked the very last 'Western' passenger train on BR — the 'Western Tribute' on 26 February 1977. Since then, the locomotive has been part of the National Collection and is normally based at the National Railway Museum in York. The pairing of *Western Fusilier* and WSR-based No D1010 *Western Campaigner* — two of the final four 'Westerns' to be withdrawn — makes a fine sight passing Castle Hill with the 4.45pm Minehead–Bishops Lydeard on 29 April 2000. *Richard Jones*

Back in black

Right: For its last season in traffic prior to overhaul, the popular BR '45xx' class 2-6-2T No 4561, owned by the West Somerset Railway Association, was repainted in BR unlined black livery, which suited the engine well and looked very smart. The ex-GWR 'Small Prairie' tank passes the site of Leigh Bridge Loop — between Stogumber and Crowcombe Heathfield — with the 2.50pm Minehead–Bishops Lydeard on 13 September 1998. No 4561 is currently on display inside the 'Gauge Museum' at Bishops Lydeard, waiting its turn for overhaul. *Steve Gooding*

'Black Five' at Doniford

Above: One of the popular Stanier 'Black Fives' — of which 842 were built between 1934 and 1951 — has spent two very successful summer seasons based on the WSR in 2000 and 2001. No 45337, built in April 1937, coasts round the curve past Doniford Halt with the 4.05pm ex Bishops Lydeard on 6 September 2001. *Peter Darke*

Approaching Crowcombe

Right: GWR '57xx' 0-6-0PT No 9681, visiting from the Dean Forest Railway, enjoyed a very successful stay on the WSR in the spring of 1998. It is here seen passing the up distant signal at Crowcombe Heathfield with the 10.15am Minehead–Bishops Lydeard in May of that year. C. B. Collett's standard design for an 0-6-0 pannier tank was first introduced in 1929, and between then and 1950 no fewer than 863 engines of the '57xx' class were built, being used for shunting and light mixed-traffic duties. No 9681 was both built and withdrawn by British Railways, in May 1949 and July 1965 respectively. The WSR would love to have one of these engines based permanently on the line! *Don Bishop*

'Thomas' and friends

Special events have become a regular and popular feature with various audiences in recent seasons — none more so than on the one weekend each season when 'Thomas the Tank Engine' and many of his friends come to visit Minehead.

Left: In glorious sunny weather, children are entertained on the platform at Minehead, as *Thomas* steams by in the background giving brake van rides during the 2001 event. On this occasion, *Thomas* is 'played' by LMS 'Jinty' 0-6-0T No 47383, from the Severn Valley Railway. The class was intended primarily for shunting and light mixed-traffic duties, with a total of 422 being built. The SVR's engine entered service in October 1926 (as LMS No 16466) and spent most of its life in the North West of England before being purchased for preservation in November 1966. It normally carries authentic BR black livery, but was repainted to serve as *Thomas* for a short period to deputise for the 'regular' *Thomas*, which was undergoing overhaul. *David Holman*

Right: "Hello there, how are you…?" On 10 July 1999 *Percy* and *Thomas* entertain at Minehead — the former shunting the Troublesome Trucks, whilst *Thomas* is again giving brake-van rides. *Thomas* is another Severn Valley-based engine — 0-6-0T No 686 *The Lady Armaghdale*, built back in 1898 by the Hunslet Engine Co of Leeds and delivered new to the Manchester Ship Canal Railway. *Percy* is one of the once-numerous Peckett 0-4-0 saddle tanks, built in Bristol — No 1788 *Kilmersdon*, which worked for many years at various Somerset coalfields in the Radstock area. Now in the care of the Somerset & Dorset Railway Trust at Washford, No 1788 was renamed *Mike Palmer* in 2000 in memory of one of the Trust's longest-serving volunteers. *Richard Jones*

Doniford stone

Left: In March 2000 the WSR was again used to transport stone in connection with a Coastal Protection Works Scheme at Helwell Bay, near Doniford. The cliffs in the area were retreating, where unprotected, and the WSR runs very close to the top of the cliff at this point. The work was therefore essential in order to safeguard the future of the WSR. Trains were again operated by EWS, with Westbury-based locomotives from Classes 59 and 66 used, hauling up to 20 MEA wagons. No 59206, one of the Class 59/2s previously operated by National Power, runs downhill past Combe Florey, north of Bishops Lydeard, with the return stone empties on 10 March 2000. *Don Bishop*

Diesels at Nethercott

No fewer than 10 heritage diesel locomotives were evident at the 1998 Diesel Gala event — including a line-up of five Class 50s and, for the first time, a 'Deltic' hauling passenger trains on the WSR.

Upper right: One of the visiting Class 50s, No 50015 *Valiant* — a former favourite of Plymouth Laira depot — passes between the trees at Nethercott with the 9.00am Minehead–Bishops Lydeard on 20 September 1998. The locomotive carries BR 'large logo' livery. *Richard Jones*

Lower right: In the very smart BR two-tone green livery, 'Deltic' No D9019 *Royal Highland Fusilier* climbs towards Crowcombe Heathfield with the 5.25pm from Bishops Lydeard later the same day. *Richard Jones*

Main-line charter

Left: A pair of well turned-out Direct Rail Services-owned Class 20s, Nos 20308 and 20311, pass the site of the former station at Norton Fitzwarren — closed in 1961 — with a Blackpool–Minehead charter train (1Z70) formed largely of chocolate-and-cream-liveried stock on 6 May 2000. DRS locomotives are relatively infrequent visitors to Taunton. The junction between the WSR and the national railway network can be seen behind the train in the right background. To date, only one other Class 20 — No D8110, based at the South Devon Railway — has traversed the Minehead branch. *Richard Jones*

Steam in the landscape

Right: GWR '2251' class 0-6-0 No 3205 was once a regular performer on the WSR but is currently based on the South Devon Railway. For a very short period in the spring of 1998 the engine, which normally runs in post-1946 Great Western livery, was temporarily turned out in later British Railways livery for a series of charter trains for photographers. Against the backdrop of the Quantock Hills, No 3205 steams past Roebuck Farm, between Crowcombe Heathfield and Stogumber, on 30 March 1998 with a once-typical branch-line milk and parcels train. The tower of Crowcombe parish church can be seen at the foot of the hills in the background. No 3205 is the only preserved engine of this class, 120 of which were ordered by the Great Western and built at Swindon between 1930 and 1948. *Don Bishop*

'Modified Hall'

Left: Two BR black-liveried ex-GWR engines visited the WSR in the spring of 1998, primarily for the Spring Steam Gala — '57xx' class 0-6-0PT No 9681 *(see page 19)* and 'Modified Hall' class 4-6-0 No 6990 *Witherslack Hall.* The latter makes a fine sight as it nears Crowcombe Heathfield towards the end of the six-mile climb from Williton with the 10.15am Minehead–Bishops Lydeard on 17 May 1998. *Richard Jones*

Leaving the coast

Above: In all, 10 engines, including six 'guests', were in steam at the Spring Steam Gala in 2001, which commemorated the WSR's 25th anniversary of train operation — the line having reopened at Easter 1976. One of the visiting engines was LNER 'B1' 4-6-0 No 61264, the first ever visit of a member of this class — or, indeed, any LNER engine — to Minehead, though the 'B1s' were once a fairly regular sight in the Bristol area on inter-regional trains. No 61264 was built by the North British Locomotive Co in Glasgow in 1947, and, following withdrawal in 1965, became the only ex-LNER engine to find its way to Barry scrapyard. Now beautifully restored, the 'B1' rounds the curve at Doniford with the 1.57pm Minehead–Bishops Lydeard on 30 March 2001. The Bristol Channel can be seen in the background — the last glimpse of the sea that passengers get from an up train. *Quentin Hawkes*

BR blue at Bicknoller

Left: Two visiting Class 50 diesel-electric locomotives, Nos D444 and 50031 *Hood* — both normally resident on the Severn Valley Railway at Kidderminster — head the 3.10pm Minehead–Bishops Lydeard past Bicknoller on 20 September 1998 during a Diesel Gala event. Fifty Class 50s were built by English Electric at Vulcan Foundry, Newton-le-Willows in 1967/8, initially to work primarily on the West Coast main line — both singly and in pairs — on Anglo-Scottish services north of the then limit of electrification at Crewe. Once the whole of the West Coast route to Glasgow was electrified, the '50s' were progressively moved from the London Midland Region to the Western Region between 1973 and 1976 to implement the elimination of the diesel-hydraulics. The Class 50s then became a regular sight on British Rail in the West of England. They were progressively withdrawn from 1987 to 1992, though several remain active. *Peter Darke*

'Growlers'

Right: Two of the diminishing number of electric-train-heat-fitted Class 37/4 locomotives, Nos 37420 *The Scottish Hosteller* and 37402 *Bont Y Bermo*, pass between the two bridges at Woolston, south of Williton, with a Preston–Minehead charter (1Z92) on 1 May 1999. The two locomotives worked the train throughout. No 37420 carries Regional Railways colours, whilst its partner is in BR Trainload Freight two-tone grey; both liveries are now obsolete and no longer normally used for repaints. Whilst many Class 37s have now been withdrawn, several are still active around the national network on both passenger and freight duties. *Richard Jones*

Stogumber

Left: The unique 0-6-0ST No 813 made two short visits to the WSR in 2001. During its second visit — for the Autumn Steam Gala — the small tank passes through Stogumber station with the 9.25am ex Minehead 'mixed' train, formed of a Mk 1 coach in BR(SR) green livery and a six-wheel milk-tank wagon. Stogumber station is unique on the WSR through being the only station on the line where the main station building is on the opposite side of the track from the platform. The engine, built by Hudswell Clarke of Leeds in 1900, was one of a small fleet of 0-6-0STs once owned by the Port Talbot Railway Co and used for the haulage of coal trains and the shunting of colliery yards on that South Wales system. No 813 later passed into GWR ownership, and saw further colliery use in Northumberland before being purchased for preservation — on the Severn Valley Railway — in August 1967. *Don Bishop*

Brake-van rides

Above: GWR '1366' class 0-6-0PT No 1369, the only preserved example of six outside-cylinder pannier tanks built at Swindon in 1934, made a short visit to the line in June 2000 for a special gala event to celebrate the 21st anniversary of the WSR's becoming Britain's longest heritage steam railway. No 1369 spent the weekend giving brake van rides on part of the Bishops Lydeard–Norton Fitzwarren section, being seen here near Dene Bridge. *David J. Williams*

Through trains

For over 10 years — the first such train ran on 16 June 1990 — a number of through trains from many places have operated on to the WSR, using the junction with the branch at Norton Fitzwarren, two miles west of Taunton station. These have seen a wide range of steam and diesel locomotives, in a variety of liveries, working to either Bishops Lydeard or right through to Minehead — including a number of types not seen on the branch in the pre-preservation era.

Far left: One of the RES-liveried fleet of Class 47/7 locomotives, No 47763, passes through Washford station on its way to Minehead with a Ffestiniog Railway Society charter on 18 April 1998.
Richard Jones

Left: Class 50 No 50050 *Fearless*, hauling a 12-coach Anglia Railways set, approaches Crowcombe Heathfield station — the summit of the WSR — with a Norwich–Minehead charter (1Z36) on 17 July 1999.
Richard Jones

A trio of 'Manors'

Right: One of the main highlights of the 1998 Autumn Steam Gala was, for the first time in preservation, a train hauled by three BR(W) 'Manor' class 4-6-0s — Nos 7820 *Dinmore Manor*, 7821 *Ditcheat Manor* and 7828 *Odney Manor*. Nos 7820 and 7828 have both been regular members of the WSR 'home' fleet since 1995, but *Ditcheat Manor* was making its preservation debut at the event after completion of its restoration at Minehead. With the three 'Manors' in numerical order, the 3.50pm Bishops Lydeard–Minehead passes through beautiful scenery at Nethercott on 13 September 1998.
Mark Wilkins

On shed

Left: Over 300 of the GWR 'Large Prairie' tank engines were built between 1909 and 1948. Several of these engines were allocated at Taunton shed until its closure in October 1964, and were regularly used on the Minehead branch. The success in preservation of No 4160 *(see page 5)* has shown how well suited the '5101' class is to the WSR, being reliable, powerful and economical. No fewer than three 'Large Prairie' tanks could be seen in action at the 2000 Autumn Steam Gala — Nos 4141, 4144 and 4160. On 10 September 2000 No 4141, normally

resident on the Llangollen Railway, poses outside the sheds at Minehead, awaiting its next turn of duty. On the left is the former station goods shed, which was the WSR's original workshop. The building behind No 4141, built to complement the other station structures, is a new, purpose-built locomotive workshop, opened in 1998. *Richard Jones*

'Castle' at Churchlands

Above: GWR 'Castle' class 4-6-0 No 5029 *Nunney Castle* passes Churchlands Bridge, on the climb from Bishops Lydeard to Crowcombe Heathfield, with a Minehead-bound train formed of six BR Mk 1 coaches in lined maroon livery on 29 March 2001. No 5029, which hauled a main-line charter to the WSR earlier that month, became the third 'Castle' to work over the line, following the visits of No 5051 *Earl Bathurst* the previous spring *(see page 9)* and No 7029 *Clun Castle (see page 51)* in 1997. *Don Bishop*

'Crompton'

Above: BRCW/Sulzer Type 3 — later BR Class 33 — No 33048 approaches Leigh Wood Crossing on 20 September 1998 with the 3.10pm Bishops Lydeard–Minehead, hauling the WSR's Class 115/117 three-car diesel multiple-unit. Introduced in 1960, a total of 98 of these locomotives — formed into three sub-classes (33/0,

33/1 and 33/2) — were built by the Birmingham Railway Carriage & Wagon Co to work primarily on the Southern Region, though in later years many also worked over Western Region metals. No 33048 was purchased for preservation on the WSR in 1997, and is one of a fleet of heritage diesels cared for by the Diesel & Electric Preservation Group, based at

Williton. It was repainted in 'all-over blue' and given its original number (D6566) to mark its 40th anniversary in 2001. The 'Crompton' — as the type is nicknamed — is used regularly on a variety of duties, including engineering trains. *Alan Randle*

Driver training

Above: For a very short period in February 1997, Mendip Rail (the rail-operating company of Foster Yeoman) used the West Somerset Railway in order to give crews from Germany practical experience of handling a Class 59 locomotive on a running line, prior to one of these locomotives' moving to

Germany for future use there. Bearing Foster Yeoman colours, No 59004 *Paul A. Hammond*, together with five of the quarry company's wagons, was used for the training exercise. The short train is here seen departing from Blue Anchor and beginning the climb of Washford Bank on 27 February 1997 on

one of the training runs. There remain 14 Class 59s based in Britain, divided into three sub-classes, their principal task being the haulage of heavy stone trains from quarries in the Mendip Hills. *Graham Perry*

Steam on the stone

Above: Following its arrival at Bishops Lydeard, and to avoid the need for a separate train movement, GWR '14xx' class 0-4-2T No 1450 — making its second visit to the WSR — was attached to the usual Class 37-hauled stone train and piloted the EWS locomotive as far as Williton on 30 March 1998. The rather bizarre combination of No 1450 and No 37885 is seen passing Nornvis Bridge, near Crowcombe — with the Class 37 undoubtedly doing most of the work! *Don Bishop*

'King' at Crowcombe

Right: Pride of the Great Western — and one of the heaviest engines ever to have traversed the Minehead branch — 'King' class 4-6-0 No 6024 *King Edward I* pauses in the sunshine at Crowcombe Heathfield station on 12 May 2001 whilst working a special dining train for the members of its owning group, the 6024 Preservation Society Ltd. The 'King' class was designed by the GWR's Chief Mechanical Engineer, C. B. Collett, to haul express-passenger trains from London Paddington to Plymouth and Wolverhampton, and 30 were built by the GWR at the famous Swindon Works from 1927 to 1930. They were a regular sight through Taunton in times gone by. No 6024 was built in 1930, and spent 32 years working for the GWR and BR before being withdrawn in 1962. It was purchased from Barry scrapyard in 1973 and returned to steam in 1989. *Richard Jones*

Branch-line goods

Left: GWR '57xx' class 0-6-0PT No 7760 steams away from Blue Anchor and begins the climb of Washford Bank with the 8.50am Minehead–Bishops Lydeard demonstration goods train on 22 March 1997, the second day of the railway's Spring Steam Gala. The pannier tank was one of 10 Great Western engines to work during the gala — the WSR's most successful special event to date, attracting 6,965 passengers. No 7760 was built by the North British Locomotive Co in December 1930 and spent the first few years of its life allocated to Plymouth Laira shed. After withdrawal by British Railways in November 1961 it worked for a few further years on London Transport — numbered L90 — mainly working engineers' trains. It is one of three '57xx' locomotives now in the care of Tyseley Locomotive Works, Birmingham, and is currently main-line certificated. *David J. Williams*

Another first

Right: Over 40 years separates the construction of these three diesel locomotives seen at Bishops Lydeard on 20 May 2000. Prominent in the centre is almost-new EWS Class 67 No 67026 — one of a class of 30 engines built in 1999/2000 by Alstom at Valencia in Spain (as sub-contractors for General Motors) and used primarily on postal trains throughout Britain; they are thus a regular sight at Taunton. The previous day, No 67026 became the first member of the class to work over the line when it worked the return leg of Pathfinder Tours' 'Capital Castles' charter from London Paddington to Minehead.

In the background, 'Hymek' Type 3 (later Class 35) diesel-hydraulic No D7017 shunts coaching stock, whilst Class 08 No D3462 rests in one of the up sidings. Both locomotives are based on the WSR at Williton in the care of the Diesel & Electric Preservation Group. No D7017 was built by Beyer Peacock (Hymek) Ltd in 1962 — one of a class of 101 built for service on the Western Region of British Railways, where it worked on a variety of duties until being withdrawn in March 1975. No D3462, built in 1957, was a member of a class which once totalled 1,193 locomotives built at several British Railways workshops from 1952 to 1962 that became the standard diesel shunting locomotive on BR. Many are still in use today throughout the country, in a wide variety of liveries! *Richard Jones*

'Large Prairie' at Washford

Above: GWR '5101' class 2-6-2T No 4144 coasts into Washford station in September 2000 with the 3.45pm train from Williton. Washford is the base of the Somerset & Dorset Railway Trust — owners of S&DJR '7F' 2-8-0 No 53808 — which has established a museum, shed and sidings at the station. No 4144 was one of two 'guest' engines that spent the 2000 summer season based on the WSR — working 2,719 miles that year — and, for a short time later that month, was one of three 'Large Prairie' tanks that could be seen working on the WSR. No 4144 was built by the GWR at Swindon in September 1946 and, after withdrawal by BR in June 1965, was purchased by the Great Western Society in 1974 — one of a large fleet of ex-GWR engines now based at Didcot Railway Centre. It was the 50th engine to depart from Barry scrapyard.

David J. Williams

Big disappointment

Above: BR Standard Class 9F 2-10-0 No 92212 stands forlornly in the down headshunt at Minehead station on 12 September 1999. One of a very successful class of 251 engines designed primarily for main-line freight duties and constructed from 1954 to 1960, No 92212 — built in September 1959 at Swindon — was hired by the WSR for the Autumn Steam Gala, but was received in poor condition from its then base, the Great Central Railway. Although it worked from Bishops Lydeard to Minehead the previous day, trailing No 7820 *Dinmore Manor* as an insurance policy, it was failed upon arrival and did not work a passenger train on the WSR. In the background is GWR '5101' class 2-6-2T No 5193, an ex-Barry scrapyard engine purchased by the WSR from its previous owner in 1999. Built in 1934, the engine is currently undergoing restoration at Minehead and will be turned out as a 2-6-0 tender engine. *Richard Jones*

Observation car

Left: Another BR/Brush/Sulzer Class 47 diesel bearing the Rail Express Systems red livery, No 47732 *Restormel*, hauls the 'Racal Belle' observation car past Nethercott — between Bishops Lydeard and Crowcombe Heathfield — on 26 May 1999 on a special corporate hospitality train. This was the railway's smallest ever through train! The saloon is of LMS design (No 999503), built by BR at Wolverton Works in 1958 and restored on the Severn Valley Railway. *Ken Steel*

'47' on the stone

Right: For the 16-month duration of the contract for transporting stone in connection with the Minehead sea-defence scheme *(see page 8)* there were only three occasions when the train was hauled by a Class 47 diesel — twice by No 47016 *Atlas* and once by No 47475. Haulage of the Minehead stone-train workings was dominated by the English Electric Class 37s. At Longlands Farm, south of Bishops Lydeard, No 47016 — bearing the now obsolete BR Railfreight grey with large logo livery — works the down loaded train (4.45pm ex Norton Fitzwarren) on 7 April 1998. The locomotive was subsequently scrapped. *Richard Jones*

Past the primroses

Left: The very impressive BR black-liveried combination of BR Standard Class 4 2-6-0 No 76079 and LMS Ivatt Class 2 2-6-2T No 41312 rounds Nethercott curve with the 3.05pm ex Bishops Lydeard on 19 March 1999 during the Spring Steam Gala. No 76079, built by British Railways at Horwich Works in February 1957, is normally based on the East Lancashire Railway but spent the 1999 season based on the WSR. No 41312 was one of a class of 130 engines built by the London, Midland & Scottish Railway and British Railways from 1946 to 1952. Hired for the 1999 Spring Gala, it proved both a popular and successful performer. It is normally based at the Mid-Hants line, but has visited several heritage steam lines. *Brian Aston*

Green 'Whistler'

Above: English Electric Type 4 — later Class 40 — No D345 rounds the curve at Doniford with an up service on 26 September 1999. This was its second appearance on the WSR, though between its visits it had been repainted from BR all-over blue to early BR green. Note the crossed-spades headboard, in recognition of its visit to the seaside! *John Swatton*

'Hall' at Eastcombe

Above: GWR 'Hall' class 4-6-0 No 4920 *Dumbleton Hall* steams well towards Eastcombe, north of Bishops Lydeard — and past the WSR's much-photographed walnut tree — on 30 March 1997 with the 4.05pm service to Minehead, shortly after arriving on the line. Owned by the South Devon Railway Trust, No 4920 is the oldest surviving 'Hall', having been built by the GWR at Swindon

Works in March 1929. It was based on the WSR between March 1997 and September 1998, and in that time ran a total of 12,170 miles, proving itself to be ideally suited to the line. Altogether, 259 'Halls' and 71 'Modified Halls' were built by the GWR and BR from 1924 to 1950, all at Swindon, and proved themselves to be superb mixed-traffic engines. *Richard Jones*

Arriving at Bishops Lydeard

Right: BR Standard Class 4 2-6-4T No 80136 coasts downhill into Platform 2 at Bishops Lydeard with a train from Minehead in April 2001. Semaphore signalling has now been fully commissioned at Bishops Lydeard by the WSR, not only aiding train operation but also adding considerably to the general period ambience of the station. *David J. Williams*

Stanier duo

Above: The WSR has been used on several occasions to stable engines used on main-line charters in the West Country, and not only those destined for Minehead. One such occasion was in the autumn of 1998, when two SVR-based former LMS engines — '8F' 2-8-0 No 48773 and 'Black Five' No 45110 — were stabled at Bishops Lydeard for a few days after working Pathfinder Tours' 'Stannary Staniers' charter on 31 October 1998, which was steam-hauled from Penzance to Taunton. The two Stanier-designed engines have been members of the Severn Valley's steam fleet for over 30 years.

The '8F' — the standard heavy-freight engine of the LMS — emerged as No 8233 from the North British Locomotive Co's Hyde Park Works, Glasgow, in August 1940 as part of a War Department order of locomotives for service in France. After an eventful career, No 48773 was one of the very last steam engines to be withdrawn by BR, in August 1968, prior to preservation. No 45110, a member of one of the most successful British locomotive classes, was built in June 1935, and was also withdrawn in August 1968, having been one of the engines used on BR's 'Farewell to Steam' tour.

On this occasion, the two engines did not work passenger trains on the WSR — though No 48773 did enjoy a very successful season on the WSR in 1993. *Jeff Treece*

'Castle' at Watersmeet

Right: The GWR 'Castle' class, designed by
C. B. Collett and introduced in 1923, formed the
backbone of express-passenger workings on the Great
Western Railway and, later, British Railways Western
Region for around 40 years. Several members of the
class have been preserved, and three of them —
Nos 5029 *Nunney Castle (see page 35)*, 5051 *Earl
Bathurst (see page 9)* and 7029 *Clun Castle* — have
worked trains on the WSR, the upgrading of the
infrastructure meaning they can now operate on the
line without restriction, whereas they were banned
from working to Minehead in GWR and BR days
because of their weight.

   Clun Castle was the second of the final batch of
'Castles' (Nos 7028-37), built at Swindon in 1950.
One of its finest moments was working an
enthusiasts' special to commemorate the end of
express-steam working on the Western Region in
1964 when, on the descent of Wellington Bank in
Somerset, it achieved a top speed of 96mph on the
fastest-ever recorded timing for steam over the
arduous route between Plymouth and Bristol. In 1965
No 7029 worked the very last BR steam service from
Paddington, before being withdrawn in December of
that year — the last 'Castle' to remain in active
service — and purchased for preservation at Tyseley
shortly thereafter.

   No 7029 was one of 10 ex-GWR engines that
worked at the 1997 Spring Steam Gala and is seen
here passing Watersmeet, shortly after departing from
Bishops Lydeard, with the 9.35am to Minehead on
22 March 1997. *Don Bishop*

Climbing to Crowcombe

Left: One of the most popular 'guest' engines to have visited the WSR in recent years has been GWR '43xx' class 2-6-0 No 7325. Several members of the class worked from Taunton over the branch lines to Barnstaple and to Minehead. No 7325 was built originally in 1932 as No 9303 at a recorded cost of £5,161, one of the last batch of engines that were specially weighted at the front end in a bid to reduce excessive tyre wear on the leading driving wheels. Withdrawn in April 1964, the engine was purchased for preservation in May 1974, one of only two '43xxs' to escape the cutter's torch. No 7325 bursts out of the rock cutting at Sampford Brett, south of Williton, as it climbs the six miles to the summit of the line at Crowcombe Heathfield with the 2.25pm Minehead–Bishops Lydeard on 26 March 2000. *Don Bishop*

Watchet departure

Right: The Southern Railway's 'West Country' class was a lighter-weight version of the earlier 'Merchant Navy' design and intended for use on those secondary routes barred to the heavier engines. A total of 110 engines was built. They were originally streamlined, but 60 of the class were rebuilt as a more conventional design from 1957. One of these rebuilt Pacifics, No 34027 *Taw Valley* — built in April 1946 as No 21C127 — spent nine years of its life working in the West Country before being withdrawn by BR in August 1964. The engine was purchased for preservation in 1980 and has worked on several heritage steam lines and on the main line.
On 28 August 1997, during the first of its two visits to the WSR, No 34027 departs from Watchet station with the 10.25am ex Bishops Lydeard, resplendent in BR lined green. *Richard Jones*

Maroon 'Western'

Left: Repainted in early BR maroon livery, which suited the class so well, 'Western' No D1010 *Western Campaigner* climbs past Water Farm, south of Stogumber, with a southbound train during the WSR 1960s Weekend in September 2000. The 'Western' class diesel-hydraulics were turned out simultaneously by the BR workshops at Swindon and Crewe from 1961 to 1964. No D1010 has been based on the WSR since 1991, and since then has carried four different liveries! *Don Bishop*

Class 66 to Minehead

Above: The General Motors Class 66 Co-Co locomotives were introduced into Britain in 1998, and over 300 are now in service with several train-operating companies. Although designed primarily for freight work — upon which they can be seen throughout the country — several have been used to haul charter trains to the WSR. The first Class 66 to work through to Minehead was No 66083, when it hauled a 14-coach train from Peterborough on 14 October 2000. In this view another English,

Welsh & Scottish Railway member of the class, No 66116, coasts downhill over Roebuck Farm curve — north of Crowcombe Heathfield — with a Hertfordshire Railtours charter from Letchworth to Minehead (1Z45) on 1 September 2001. *Peter Darke*

The 'Quantock Flyer II'

The Mid-Hants Railway's 'Green Train' has made two very successful visits to the WSR — on 20 March 1999 and 9 September 2000, behind BR Standard Class 5 4-6-0 No 73096 and SR Bulleid Pacific No 34016 *Bodmin* respectively. Whilst No 73096 had already worked a passenger train on the line before — as a 'guest' at the March 1996 Somerset & Dorset Gala — this was *Bodmin*'s first visit of to the WSR.

Top left: A member of the Southern Railway's 'West Country' class, *Bodmin* rests beside the water tower at Bishops Lydeard on 9 September 2000 — during the Autumn Steam Gala — after arrival with the 'Quantock Flyer II'. The nine-coach train was worked from Bishops Lydeard to Minehead by two GWR 2-6-2Ts, Nos 4144 and 4160. No 34016 emerged from Brighton Works in November 1945, as No 21C116. It was a regular sight in the West Country during the first 12 years of its life, working from Exmouth Junction shed. Withdrawn in June 1964, the engine was purchased for preservation in 1972 and returned to steam on the MHR in 1979. *John Swatton*

Bottom left: The return leg of the 'Quantock Flyer II' charter on the WSR was worked by GWR '2251' class 0-6-0 No 3205 *(see page 25)* and another SR 'West Country' 4-6-2, No 34027, in its 'Hogwarts Express' red livery *(see page 6)*. The unusual combination pass Bicknoller, south of Stogumber. No 34027 — whose 'real' name is *Taw Valley (see page 53)* — spent the 2000 summer season based on the line, whilst No 3205, a former WSR resident, was a 'guest' at the Autumn Gala. In total, the charter was worked by five different steam engines, plus an EWS Class 37 diesel between Bishops Lydeard and Westbury. *Peter Darke*

Type 2 trio

Above: No fewer than 263 Brush Type 2 diesel locomotives — later Class 31 — were built by Brush Traction at Loughborough from 1957 to 1962 and were the first main-line diesels allocated to BR's Eastern Region. They worked on a variety of passenger and freight duties, and in later years worked further afield, many being allocated to the Western Region, where they were not well liked at

first because they hastened the decline of the popular 'Hymek' diesel-hydraulics. The last few surviving members of the class were withdrawn by EWS in 2000, but many are still active on the national network and on heritage railways.

On 28 June 1997, two of the final EWS survivors, Nos 31466 and 31420 — in contrasting liveries — double-headed a Pathfinder Tours charter from York

to Minehead, which they worked throughout. This provided the unusual sight of main-line diesels being refuelled at Minehead. On the return working, the two Class 31s were piloted by WSR-based Class 25 No D7523 between Minehead and Williton. The triple-header enters the up platform at Williton — the principal crossing place on the line — prior to the Class 25's removal. *Graham Perry*

Unsung hero

Left: One of the less-photographed aspects of the WSR over the years have been the diesel multiple-units, which have been a regular sight on the line ever since it reopened in 1976. Whilst the use of diesel railcars has declined gradually since then, they still have a valuable role to play and still feature regularly on train services. In recent years, services have been worked by a small fleet of Class 115/117 vehicles that are now enjoying a new lease of life. On 16 August 1997 a three-car set coasts into the up platform at the very picturesque station at Blue Anchor with the 2.55pm Minehead–Williton. *Bryan Hicks*

Leaving Lydeard

Right: The London, Midland & Scottish Railway Class 5, designed by William Stanier, was introduced in 1934 and over three decades established itself as a powerful mixed-traffic locomotive, proving equally at home on passenger and goods trains. Members of the class were a regular sight over many parts of the rail network, and could be seen in the North West of England right up until the end of steam on BR in 1968. No 45337 was completed in April 1937 and, following withdrawal in February 1965, became one of six 'Black Fives' that ended up at Barry scrapyard. After purchase for preservation, it was returned to steam at Bury. No 45337 has enjoyed two very successful seasons working trains on the line — in 2000 and 2001 — to support the regular steam fleet, achieving a total WSR mileage of 6,553. Here, the 'Black Five' tackles the climb away from Bishops Lydeard and approaches the footpath crossing at Whisky Trail with the 10.25am to Minehead on 22 August 2001. *Richard Jones*

Vintage Great Western

Left: GWR 0-6-0PT No 6412, owned by the WSR Association, has been a regular sight on the line since it reopened in 1976. After its last overhaul, completed in 1998, the engine was returned to steam in early Great Western plain green livery, complete with the 'shirt button' monogram on its tank sides. In a scene that has a pure 1930s feel to it, No 6412 coasts downhill past Churchlands, between Crowcombe Heathfield and Bishops Lydeard, with the 3.00pm ex Minehead on 26 March 2000, complete with two genuine Great Western carriages in tow.
Richard Jones

Vintage 1960s!

Left: In complete contrast, GWR 'Manor' class 4-6-0 No 7828 *Odney Manor* was turned out to reflect the general condition of engines in the later days of steam on British Railways for the 1960s Weekend in September 2000. The 'Manor' — without its name and number plates — is here seen awaiting its next turn of duty at Bishops Lydeard. *Richard Jones*

Standard '4' at Kentsford

Above: The visit of British Railways Standard Class 4 2-6-0 No 76079 for almost the whole 1999 season proved how ideally suited the type is to working on the WSR, even though members of the class were never seen on the branch in the BR era. Altogether, 115 engines were built at two BR workshops — Horwich and Doncaster and — from 1952 to 1957, and were used principally on the Southern and Midland Regions. No 76079 — built at Horwich in 1957, spending all its BR working life based in the North West of England and withdrawn just 10 years later — passes Kentsford, on the climb from Watchet to Washford, with the 10.25am ex Bishops Lydeard on 11 April 1999. *David Holman*

The 'Royal Duchy'

Left: GWR 'King' class 4-6-0 No 6024 *King Edward I* makes a fine sight as it rounds Nethercott curve, between Bishops Lydeard and Crowcombe Heathfield, on 22 March 2000 with a special photographers' charter train. The engine is always turned out in immaculate condition — a tribute to its hard-working support crew — and has enjoyed several short stays on the WSR in between its main-line charter commitments. *Steve Gooding*

Diesel double

Above: Four heritage diesel locomotives visited the WSR in the autumn of 1999 to take part in a special Diesel Gala Weekend. Two of them — Class 46 No D172 *Ixion* and Class 24 No D5054 — approach Nornvis Bridge, south of Crowcombe Heathfield, with the 3.10pm Bishops Lydeard–Minehead on 24 September 1999. No D172 is main-line-certificated and based at Crewe, whilst the '24' is one of a large fleet of heritage diesels at the East Lancashire Railway. *Richard Jones*

And finally…

Overleaf: Whilst the engine — GWR 'Manor' class 4-6-0 No 7820 *Dinmore Manor* — was featured in the first *Locomotives of the West Somerset Railway* book, the opportunity of including a photograph of steam in the snow — a rare combination in West Somerset — was too good to miss! No 7820, the first of the last batch of 'Manors' built, in 1950, passes Nethercott with the 12.25pm ex Bishops Lydeard on 30 December 2000. *Richard Jones*